BOOK DESCRIPTION

This book is about socialism and how to work to bring it about in the United States. Usually such treatises are highly abstract, but I have chosen to draw some conclusions based on the experiences of my own life. I was radicalized by the Vietnam War, and I wholeheartedly followed "Marxism-Leninism" for many years as a budding revolutionary. I have finally come to realize that classical Marxism has some fundamental weaknesses, and in particular that the Leninist notion of a vanguard party to implement a "proletarian dictatorship" over society is incompatible with socialism. Thus salient experiences of my life are summarized in Chapter 1.

Chapter 2 presents the theory of dialectical materialism as reformulated by me in another work; this methodology is necessary, I think, in order to understand the (dialectical) development of society.

In Chapter 3 I discuss Leninism, rejecting the concept of the one-party dictatorship and examining the role of democracy in social organization; what is crucial is the (democratic) self-organization of people seeking to effect progressive social change, with socialist organizations helping to tie together various struggles and keeping people's eyes on the prize, but not trying to control these struggles.

Chapter 4 examines the question of who shall bring about socialism, rejecting the classical Marxist formulation that the increasingly immiserated working class will simply overthrow capitalism and thereby rule society. A major role in achieving socialism must also be played by the "middle class" and by non-economic struggles for a decent life. The fact that we are *all* basically irrational beings must also be taken into consideration.

Finally, Chapter 5 presents a model of socialist economy proposed by the British intellectual Ralph Miliband: "A socialized economy would consist of three distinct sectors. First, there would be a predominant and varied public sector. Secondly, there would exist a substantial and expanding cooperative sector. Thirdly, there would endure a sizeable privately owned sector, mainly made up of small and medium firms, with an important part to play in the provision of goods, services, and amenities." Since significant private enterprise is to be allowed indefinitely in this model, it may seem to be a version of social democracy, but it makes the crucial difference of requiring the "commanding heights of the economy" (banks, big corporations, etc.) to be state owned (*i.e.*, in the public sector). The chapter concludes with a rational, absolutely compelling argument for replacing capitalism with socialism.

BEYOND CLASSICAL MARXISM

Dave Jette
April 18, 2020

Dedicated to the memory of the many millions of people who perished under the Soviet Union's "socialist" one-party system.

CONTENTS

This book is available from Lulu.com, in soft-cover ($9) and hard-cover ($19) editions.

The author, living in Seattle, can be contacted at dave@jettes.org.

PREFACE

This book is about socialism and how to work to bring it about in the United States. Usually such treatises are highly abstract, but I have chosen to draw some conclusions based on the experiences of my own life. (I am now 77 years old and have actually led two lives, one in leftist politics and the other an academic career.) Thus to some extent the content of this book is anecdotal, for most everyone has some tale to tell. However, I think that this method will be effective in bringing out the points that I wish to make.

Thus we begin, in Chapter 1, with an outline of my life; its particular relevance will become apparent in Chapter 4. Chapter 2 presents the theory of dialectical materialism, which is essential for understanding the development of human society. Chapter 3 is on organization, starting with Leninism (a top-down "vanguard party" orientation with which I was imbued at first for many years) and concluding with the necessity of following a more democratic, bottom-up path to socialism. Chapter 4 addresses the question of who shall be the agents of progressive social transformation – not simply the increasingly oppressed working class with nothing to lose but their chains, as Marx and Engels observed in nineteenth century Europe. Finally, Chapter 5 presents a model of socialist economy and why it is not only desirable but even imperative for us to strive for this.

CHAPTER 1. TWO LIVES

a. Childhood

My father was rather conservative, but very strong on civil rights. He worked in an executive capacity for private social service funding organizations in a number of cities ("United Fund", the capitalists' answer to government funding of social services). My mother was a liberal pacifist, and she tried to inculcate me to never defend myself against violence. She functioned as a housewife, servicing at least once as a PTA president, until she became a social worker after I graduated from high school.

When I was in the first through fourth school grades in New Haven (1948-1952), my family was living in a housing project which was segregated into white and Black components. After living for awhile in the white section, my parents demanded to know why such segregation occurred, and they were told that we were welcome to move into the Black section. And this we did. The only name I remember from that early time is that of my best friend, who was Black, of course.

In 1952 we moved to Savannah, Georgia and I got a taste of real segregation (separate water fountains, for example!). I had essentially no contact with Black people there, but I understand that my parents were members of the local NAACP. It was there that I started my electronics hobby, and I taught myself to fix television sets.

In the middle of my eighth grade we moved to Pawtucket, Rhode Island, but my father didn't last long there: as head of the United Fund, he refused to allow the YMCA to continue to control this organization for its own benefit. So I spent tenth through twelfth grades in Stamford, Connecticut. Stamford High School had many Black students, but I had very little contact with them since they were practically all in the lower class divisions. One person whom I did know, however, was my (white) friend Joe Lieberman[1]. I did start an extracurricular philosophy club while there, and I graduated with the honor of being named, in the yearbook, as the best mathematics student.

I spent my four years of undergraduate study at Cornell University, 1960-1964, and it was there, associating for the first time with radicals, that I began my transformation from a liberal to a radical. I joined, and became president of, Watermargin, a fraternal living house (not one of the ubiquitous Greek "fraternity houses") which had been founded by liberal-minded World War II veterans.

At Cornell I concentrated on learning physics and mathematics, and I took a special advanced mathematics course for three semesters. This course started off with about 25 high-ranking mathematics students, but by its third semester we were down to six or seven students, three of whom were "A" students. I was one of these "A" students, and another was Paul Wolfowitz[2]. The surprising thing about Wolfowitz was that he was still in high school – truly a brilliant person! (This fact will be relevant in Chapter 4.)

I was starting to understand how the real world works, reading the *National Guardian* and *I.F Stone's Weekly*. However, I remained a liberal while at Cornell. I recall going to a speech on campus by Malcolm X, and remarking afterwards to a friend that he was "crazy". (My friend immediately contradicted this assertion.) I was most fortunate to have witnessed in person Martin Luther King Jr.'s famous "I have a dream" speech, and I recall thinking that his speech and that of John Lewis (of SNCC) were the (only) two outstanding ones at the August 1963 March on Washington for Jobs and Freedom. The Kennedy assassination[3] in November 1963 greatly disturbed me, for as a physicist I knew that the official story couldn't possibly be true. Even more disturbing was the escalating Vietnam War, and I signed a statement, published in May 1964 in the *New York Herald Tribune*, that I would refuse to fight in Vietnam "for the suppression of the Vietnamese struggle for national independence". (This statement is given as Appendix A.)

During the summer of 1964 ("Freedom Summer") I did Black voter registration in Fayette

County, Tennessee which, bordering Mississippi, was one of the two remaining counties in Tennessee that could be considered to be "Deep South". This project was to be partially funded by (Cornell) student dues, and there was strong opposition among the students to such funding; a referendum among the students was held, and (surprisingly) the funding was approved. (A portent of things to come, regarding student activism!) Joining the Cornell contingent was a large group of persons from New York City, and I subsequently deduced from circumstantial evidence that this had probably been a clandestine Communist Party project.

b. Radicalized

I spent the next three years obtaining a Master's degree in physics at Brandeis University under a National Science Foundation scholarship. This was a time when I was finally radicalized by the Vietnam War (specifically, by its sharp escalation in February 1965) and by Malcolm's assassination in that same month. I just *had* to do something with my life, beyond a normal academic career. I was strongly attracted to the (then-)Maoist Progressive Labor Party ("PL"), and although I never joined it, I did at least get myself ejected and arrested at the HUAC hearings for creating a disturbance in support of the in-your-face testimony by some PL leaders.

At this time I was reading about the amazing human progress being made in China, in books such as

Fanshen by William Hinton and **The Other Side of the River** by Edgar Snow. Further, the Great Proletarian Cultural Revolution was raging in China under Chairman Mao's direction, promising to rid the country of capitalist-road leaders. I regarded my scientific ability as being first-rate, and my future became obvious: I would go to Canada to concentrate fully on obtaining my Ph.D. degree (without having to deal with distracting PL activity), and then move to China to support their building a socialist country, as a scientist.

So I spent the next three years earning my Ph.D. degree in theoretical physics at the University of Calgary, completely inactive politically except for applying to move to China. I received my degree at the end of 1970 and moved to Vancouver awaiting word back from China (which never came). In the fall of 1971 I joined the Partisan Organization, a self-styled revolutionary organization of some 25 members, and, as is my wont, I quickly rose to leadership in it.

But in the fall of 1992 the Partisans incredibly committed hari-kari by disbanding in order to join the Communist Party of Canada (Marxist-Leninist). The six-person Central Committee of the Partisan Organization figured out that the Partisans were actually already a party of the vanguard Party, that it was in fact just its "unorganized tendency" while CPC(M-L) was it "organized tendency". I am most embarrassed to have played such an active role in railroading the Partisan Organization's demise through the organization[4].

Far more embarrassing was my political naivete in trying to join CPC(M-L), which was an utter caricature of a Leninist party. (For example, one issue of their national newspaper started off with "Blood Debts Must Be Paid in Blood!" in large red letters.) I had applied to join in November 1972, but by January I had had enough, having been thoroughly trashed at a branch meeting for circulating a twelve-page paper entitled "Overthrow the Bourgeois Reactionary Line in Vancouver" which thoroughly criticized local political work. (Yes, I had gone whole-hog in accepting the polemical methods of CPC(M-L) and yes, I could write these lengthy polemics with the best of them.) I then wrote and circulated a paper entitled "The Communist Party of Canada (Marxist-Leninist) vs. 'The Scum of the Earth' [referring to myself]" which included my original paper and thoroughly lambasted CPC(M-L). The organization replied exposing me as "the Anti-Marxist-Leninist", covering six 11"x17" pages of tiny print in their national newspaper. And so ended my pretentions of joining the vanguard party!

Now alone, I did what was to be expected of budding middle-class revolutionaries: I started working in a sawmill as an unskilled laborer (on the "green chain"), and this lasted – rather unproductively – for two years before I decided to go back to the U.S. to start a new life. But in spite of my unfortunate experiences in Vancouver, I remained psychologically committed to advancing the Revolution. My state of mind at that time is well indicated by the poem which comprises Appendix B.

c. Back in the U.S.

Living in Chicago from 1976 to 1983, I got involved in various minor political projects, and then my wife and I moved to Seattle, where we've lived ever since. For the past two decades I've been quite active in the Green Party at the local, state, and national levels, serving as treasurer and secretary. This activity with the Greens and other progressive organizations is listed at the end of my book **A Reformulation of Dialectical Materialism**[5].

One political experience in Seattle worth relating concerns the Rainbow Coalition initiated in the 1980's by Jesse Jackson. In the aftermath of the 1988 presidential election, the Washington State Rainbow Coalition was formed with about 1000 members. I was elected the state Corresponding Secretary, joining seven others to comprise the WSRC Executive Committee. On March 3, 1989 I attended a meeting of the National Rainbow Coalition in Chicago as an invited representative of the WSRC. There Jackson laid out a plan, which was duly approved, to essentially transform the state Rainbow chapters into his personal campaign committee. The new National Rainbow Coalition was to be a completely top-down organization, with the NRC president (Jackson) able to appoint and remove chapter officers, determine the operating procedures of chapters, and reorganize, suspend, or terminate any state or Congressional District chapter. I don't begrudge Jackson's wanting to convert the Rainbow Coalition for personal use, for he had created the organization in the first place, but what was abhorrent was the reaction of the WSRC leadership to this travesty of democratic functioning in what we were hoping to build.

As soon as I got back from Chicago, I gave a written report to the WSRC Executive Committee which explained in full detail what Jackson was intent on doing. To my amazement, there was no stated opposition (except mine) to the planned transformation of the National Rainbow Coalition. One ExCom member even stated that she would never circulate my report to *her* constituents! (She was a member of the Communist Party, but I don't believe any of the other ExCom members were in socialist organizations.) The ExCom evidently didn't want to do anything about the coming transformation of the WSRC, so I did the only honorable thing: as Corresponding Secretary, I maintained the organization's mailing list, so I mailed out my report to the officers of all the chapters. This action didn't bode too well with the ExCom (sorry, my bad!), but amid the furor there was nothing they could do but hold an organization-wide meeting to discuss the matter. At that meeting they presented a majority report and I countered with a detailed minority report, and I had managed to spike the liquidation of the WSRC into Jackson's transformed National Rainbow Coalition.

As mentioned above, in 1976 I moved to Chicago to start a new life (and with a new wife, Cecile Disenhouse, who has endured me to this day!). I was most fortunate to stumble on the field of medical physics, and after two years of a postdoctoral fellowship from the National Institutes of Health I was able to build an academic career in that field at a major medical university in Chicago, as summarized at the end of my book[3]. I should just mention here that I retired as a full Professor of Medical Physics at Rush University, having published 32 research papers in peer-review medical physics journals and mentored three Ph.D. students. (Two of these papers received an award as the best paper published that year in the main medical physics journal.) My research has been fully rewarding, concerning improving the treatment of cancer using radiation beams, and I was considered internationally by my colleagues as being an expert in my particular research field. (One indication of this is that I wrote a chapter in an authoritative book on various aspects of radiation therapy physics[6].) So I've actually led two lives, although my political life has always been what was most important to me.

CHAPTER 2. DIALECTICAL MATERIALISM

a. Materialism

"In the social production of their existence, men inevitably enter into definite relations, which are independent of their will, namely relations of production appropriate to a given stage in the development of their material forces of production. The totality of these relations of production constitutes the economic structure of society, the real foundation, on which arises a legal and political superstructure and to which correspond definite forms of social consciousness. The mode of production of material life conditions the general process of social, political, and intellectual life. It is not the consciousness of men that determines their existence, but their social existence that determines their consciousness. At a certain stage of development, the material productive forces come into conflict with the existing relations of production or – this merely expresses the same thing in legal terms – with the property relations within the framework of which they have operated hitherto. From forms of development of the productive forces these relations turn into their fetters. Then begins an era of social revolution. The changes in the economic foundation lead sooner or later to the transformation of the whole immense superstructure.[7]"

Thus does Marx lay out the theory of historical materialism: it is the economic system which determines current ideas ("materialism"), and not the other way around ("idealism").

But is this rigorously true? It evidently is, in stable times for a society. But when society undergoes fundamental transformation, is it not ideas which come to the forefront – ideas about what ought to be, about what can be? What are the limitations, and role, of ideas in effecting possible social change? To better understand such matters, it is useful to place social change in the context of dialectical development.

b. Dialectical development

My book, **A Reformulation of Dialectical Materialism**[5], incorporates feminist theory into the traditional Marxist presentation of the science of dialectical materialism. Doing this requires a clear understanding of dialectical development, and pages 24-44 accordingly present an enhanced scheme of human society. We shall not here go into great detail about this scheme, but refer the reader to the book and to a figure (also given here) which depicts the scheme as follows.

Society is organized most broadly as an inner circle (the "Shell of Being") surrounded by a "Shell of Consciousness". The inner shell is relevant to materialism, while the outer shell concerns idealism. Each of these shells is divided into adjacent halves, with one half concerning personal interactions (individualism, informed by feminist theory) and the other with social interactions (collectivism, starting from traditional Marxist theory). Within the Personal Half-Sphere are (from center out) the categories of Biological, Personal, and Family within the Shell of Being) and those of Emotions and Rational Thought within the Shell of Consciousness. Within the Social Half-Sphere (again from center out) are the categories of Economy, Community, and Political within the Shell of Being and those of Ideology and Science within the Shell of Consciousness.

There are definite relations among all these categories which make useful an analysis of what is possible and what is not possible in influencing the development of human society. The point is that, in a quiescent state, a half-shell below (farther from the center) another half-shell "determines" what takes place in that higher half-shell; this is exactly what Marx's materialism says, in viewing the economy as determining the "whole immense superstructure" (in the figure, the half-shells of Community, Political, Ideology, and Science in the Social Half-Sphere).

However, here is where dialectical development comes in. A higher half-shell can transform a half-shell below it when it (the higher half-shell) is dominant, resulting in a qualitatively new lower half-shell which becomes dominant in a new quiescent state. Furthermore, for this to occur, any half-shells

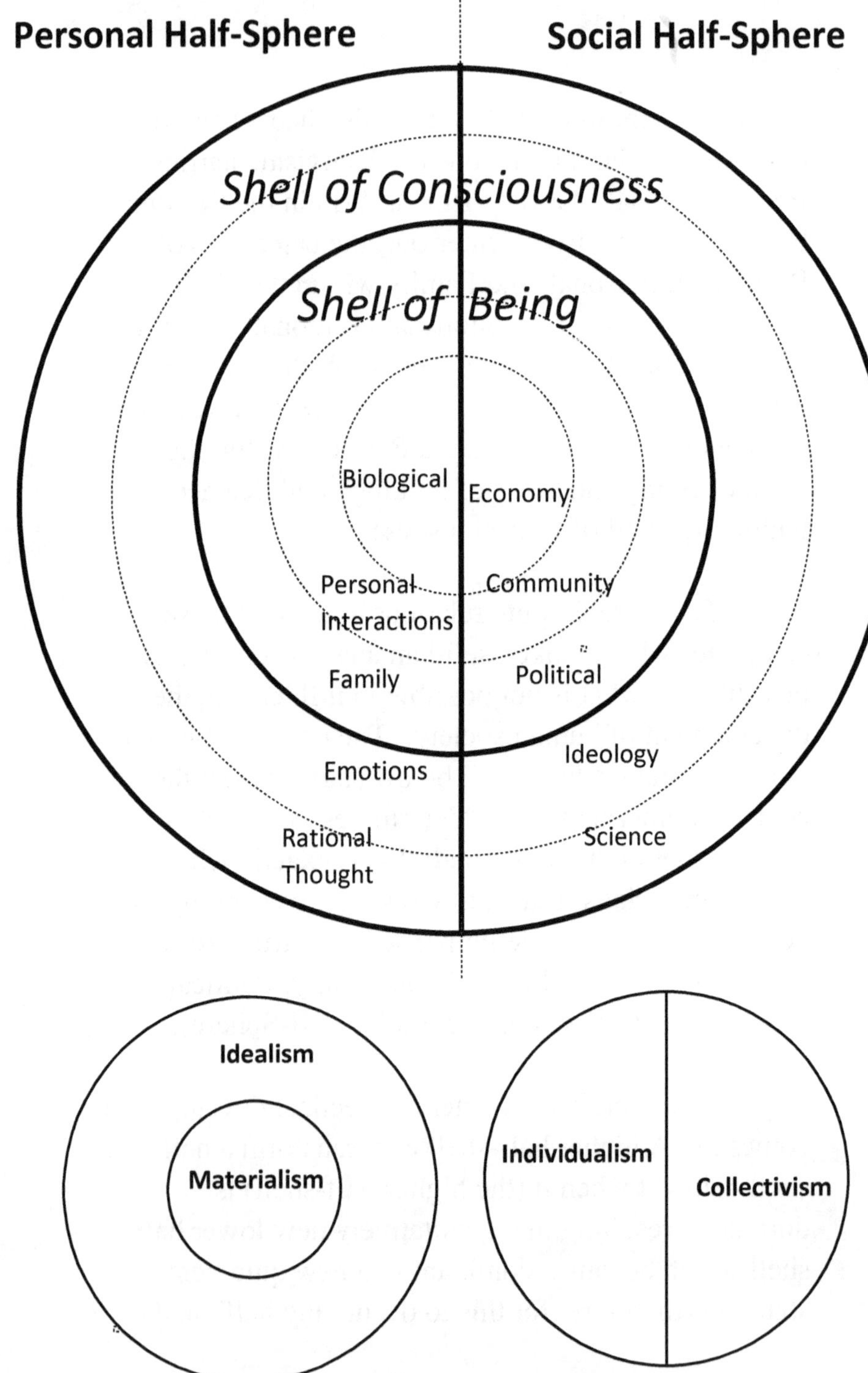
Personal Half-Sphere
Social Half-Sphere
Shell of Consciousness
Shell of Being
Biological
Economy
Personal Interactions
Community
Family
Political
Emotions
Ideology
Rational Thought
Science
Idealism
Materialism
Individualism
Collectivism

between the lower and higher ones under consideration must also be destabilized and transformed.

However, here is where dialectical development comes in. A higher half-shell can transform a half-shell below it when it (the higher half-shell) is dominant, resulting in a qualitatively new lower half-shell which becomes dominant in a new quiescent state. Furthermore, for this to occur, any half-shells between the lower and higher ones under consideration must also be destabilized and transformed.

Thus, for example, the Politics half-shell may possibly become dominant and transform the Economy (the goal of socialists who are not beholden to economic determinism!), but this will also entail a transformation of the Community half-shell. The dominance of the Political half-shell is inherently unstable (since it is so far from the center, in this scheme), so we have an example of the law of dialectics called the "negation of the negation": the ascendancy of the Politics half-shell "negates" the quiescent dominance of the Economy half-shell, but when the Economy regains its dominance, it has been transformed into a "higher" (by definition) state – "the negation of the negation".

This dialectics scheme presented here has all sorts of possibilities for understanding the development of human society. For example, the part of the Shell of Consciousness in the Social Half-

Sphere consists of the Ideology and Science half-shells, with the Ideology half-shell being below the Science half-shell. And is it not true that, in human history, ideology has usually dominated science? (Think religion, or the rejection by mindless Trump supporters of science!) Furthermore, there are various possibilities for lateral influences within the scheme, between half-shells of the Personal Half-Sphere and those of the Social Half-Sphere.

It is certainly useful (and mandatory!) that this scheme accurately depicts Marx's materialism; indeed, this is the meaning of the Shell of Being's being below the Shell of Consciousness. Of particular interest to the present study is that, in the Personal Half-Sphere, the Emotions half-shell is below the Rational Thought half-shell. This is an expression of the thesis, to be developed in Chapter 4, that we *all* are fundamentally irrational beings, subject overwhelmingly to our emotions in determining what we do, although at times rational thought can gain dominance and transform these emotions.

CHAPTER 3. ORGANIZATION

a. Leninism

Under Lenin's leadership, the Bolshevik faction of the Russian Social Democratic Labor Party (RSDLP) took power in Russia in November 1917 (the "October Revolution", according to the old-style calendar). There followed a two-year civil war with the anti-communists aided by the various capitalist countries, including the U.S. However, the Bolsheviks emerged victorious, at the cost of suppression of all other parties, particularly of the Menshevik side of the RSDLP and the Socialist Revolutionary Party (the main party of the peasantry, who constituted the huge majority of Russians). The working class, which was supposed to be in control of the state, was also suppressed as this dictatorship grew. After Lenin's death in 1924, Stalin step-by-step gained control of the Communist Party of the Soviet Union, as the Bolsheviks called themselves; he ousted Trotsky in 1927 and finally had him assassinated in 1940, and through the purge trials of 1936-1938 he had *all* of the remaining Old Bolsheviks killed, thereby giving himself absolute power. Stalin's outrageous criminal activity was finally exposed by Khrushchev in 1956.

The Soviet Union presented itself, highly inspirationally, as *the* socialist alternative to capitalism, and anti-capitalist revolutionaries in other countries followed its "vanguard party" approach which often resulted in viable one-party dictatorships (China especially, but also Vietnam, Cuba, Cambodia, Laos, and certain Eastern Europe countries). China and Cuba were particularly inspirational for the "vanguard parties" arising in the New Communist Movement in the United States in the late 1960's and 1970's[8]. Except for the followers of Trotsky, Stalin's heinous crimes were basically ignored because the result was a state which could challenge worldwide capitalism.

But a Leninist one-party dictatorship is not socialism. The essence of socialism is democracy, both politically and in the organization of the economy. Nonetheless, budding revolutionaries (myself included) latched onto Leninism as the way to go in superseding capitalism; lip-service was always given to the goal of a state democratically controlled by the working class.

b. Democracy in organization

Revolutionary parties following the Stalinist model of Leninism are necessarily top-down and completely undemocratic, but those following Trotsky at least make an honest effort to incorporate inner-party democracy, often allowing the existence of organized factions within the party (which is anathema to Stalinists!). Whether they just pretend to be democratic or really try to be democratic, all these parties arising from Leninism institute "democratic centralism", which is meant to ensure that in its political work the party functions as one, for effectiveness. The idea is that political work is decided in a democratic way by all the members of the party, through discussion leading to decision-making at a meeting of representatives of all the party units. But once the decision is formulated, everyone is expected to carry it out and not organize (at that time) in opposition to doing this.

I have no objection in principle to a party's organizing itself along democratic centralist lines, so long as it doesn't fall into the vanguardist trap of seeking to control or absorb all "truly socialist" organizations and individuals for the sake of the Revolution. I don't think that this method of organization is of great use in the present conditions of the U.S., but if they think democratic centralism will substantially increase their effectiveness, let them do it, and all the more power to them!

A case in point is the Trotskyist organization Socialist Alternative, whose member Kshama Sawant has been elected to the Seattle City Council three times now. This is no small achievement – almost a million dollars was spent to take her down in the last election, and evidently she is the highest-ranking outright socialist in office in the U.S. Sawant has been outstanding as a City Council member, but in the past she has had to follow orders from the national leadership of Socialist Alternative concerning her vote on a police commissioner and the makeup of her office staff. While I would expect her to give full consideration to the opinion of her organization, I would also expect her to do what she feels is most appropriate for her constituents. Thus I would want democratic centralism to be relaxed for a party's officeholders.

But in any case, I feel that at this time in the U.S. what is crucial is the (democratic) self-organization of people seeking to effect progressive social change. Parties can play an important role in this process, by helping to tie together various struggles and keeping people's eyes on the prize, but they must not try to control these struggles. At this stage, "bottom-up" political organizing is primary.

CHAPTER 4. AGENTS OF SOCIALIST TRANSFORMATION

a. Democracy

Democracy is at the core of the sort of "socialist" society which we aim to create. The great German socialist fighter Rosa Luxemburg stated this clearly in September 1918, when the Bolsheviks were starting to transform their revolution into a dictatorship over the masses parading itself as the "dictatorship of the proletariat":

"All this shows that 'the cumbersome mechanism of democratic institutions' possesses a powerful corrective – namely, the living movement of the masses, their unending pressure. And the more democratic the institutions, the livelier and stronger the pulse-beat of the political life of the masses, the more direct and complete is their influence – despite rigid party banners, outgrown tickets (electoral lists), etc. To be sure, every democratic institution has its limits and shortcomings, things which it doubtless shares with all other human institutions. But the remedy which Trotsky and Lenin have found, the elimination of democracy as such, is worse than the disease it is supposed to cure; for it stops up the very living source from which alone can come the correction of all the innate shortcomings of social institutions. That source is the active, untrammeled, energetic political life of the broadest masses of the people.[9]"

But in fact, there is a rationally compelling reason for seeking the overthrow of capitalism: the impending environmental catastrophe caused by anthropomorphic climate change. Capitalism by its very nature must produce more and more goods, unrestrainedly, and through its political domination of society it can and will ensure that there are no major barriers to its economic activity. Under capitalism there is no hope for our future, and the only alternative is to supersede it with socialism.

"Democracy" means exactly that: the equal right of everyone to participate in decision-making affecting their lives. It is *not*, as Leninism teaches us, the dictatorship of the working class over the rest of society (which in practice has actually meant the dictatorship of the Party over the working class and everyone else in society). People must be able to organize to advance their own interests, so long as this doesn't involve oppressing others. (No, there is not the "right" to oppress LBGTQ people, although such activity will hopefully be countered effectively in a non-oppressive way.) It must be possible to vote a given government out of power, if so desired by the majority. Of course, we cannot allow the wealthy to unduly influence political campaigns; strict campaign contribution limits must be invoked and public funding of electoral campaigns should be created. (A start at such public funding has already taken place in Seattle, with all voters provided with four $25 vouchers which can be contributed to candidates who set a limit on their campaign spending.)

Most importantly, society must take control of the "commanding heights of the economy" (banks, big corporations, etc.) through state ownership of these economic entities. (This is explained in the model of socialism presented in Chapter 5; it is in fact what crucially distinguishes socialism from social democracy.) Small-scale private enterprise is to be allowed to continue indefinitely in the new socialist society, but no longer will the bourgeoisie be able to dominate politically simply through ownership of the means of production. To a much greater extent than now, it will be "one person, one vote" rather than "one dollar, one vote".

b. People

So we are clear on the need for democracy, but exactly who is going to bring about socialism in our country, as a matter of conscious need?   Marx in middle nineteenth century Europe observed the increasing immiseration of the working class, with "nothing to lose but its chains", and postulated its providing the instrument for the eradication of capitalism through necessary class struggle. But can we say that this is true of the U.S. working class these days? Certainly workers here have been engaged in sharp struggle to defend themselves, such as the recent teachers' strikes and currently protection against the coronavirus; there should be no doubt that they have the capacity to engage in conscious class struggle, given appropriate motivation and information. And in France, another advanced capitalist country, we have the examples of the strikes in 1968 which almost brought down the whole edifice of government, and the current "yellow vest" actions.

But we also have here the phenomenon that Trump has the constant blind support of some 40% of the populace no matter how outrageous and evil his actions are. He has harnessed white supremacy, conservative Christianity, homophobia, anti-immigrant prejudice, and anti-science ideology to his campaign wagon. His supporters include a vast number of ordinary workers, and the question we should ask of them is not are they going to support the struggle to overthrow capitalism, but rather whether they are going to support his drive towards an authoritarian society, even fascism. (A discussion of fascism and Trump's laying the groundwork for such in the U.S. is given in Appendices C and D.)

Marx's conception of dialectical materialism didn't go beyond the base-superstructure dialectic quoted at the beginning of Chapter 2, and we have since been saddled with the prescription that we must always be focused on the working class's potential for overthrowing capitalism. Thus, for so many years many socialists virtually ignored non-economic struggles (against racism, for reproductive rights and against other oppression of women, against homophobia, etc.) with the rationalization that all these problems would be solved under socialism. And of course, who better to lead the working class to victory over the bourgeoisie than the Leninist vanguard party?

But humans and their societal development are much more complicated than depicted by classical Marxism, and the figure for dialectical materialism given in Chapter 2 may provide some guidance for sorting things out. Our point is that it is not just the working class, but also many members of the amorphous middle class (and conceivably some renegades from the bourgeoisie) who may struggle to achieve our envisioned socialist society. Such struggles must be "from the ground up", and it is the job of socialists not to try to control them but rather to give them impetus to work toward an overall progressive transformation of society. Socialism can be achieved only when the bulk of the working class, and many of the middle class, work together to this end.

c. Irrationality

We emphasize that we must always potentially contend with irrationality and bad politics flowing therefrom. In Chapter 2 the usual primacy of emotions over rational thought was stated and appropriately integrated into its figure for dialectical materialism. There is nothing we can do about this fact of life, other than being always on guard against irrationality and seeking to overcome it with rational thought.

My own experiences demonstrate how predominant irrationality can be even in a seemingly highly rational person. I was able to lead a highly successful academic career, with research concentrated on developing theoretical physics for application to medical treatment. Nonetheless, I really went off the deep end in Vancouver, with my role in liquidation of the Partisan Organization and my initial adulation of the ludicrous Communist Party of Canada (Marxist-Leninist). And even after these experiences it took me an embarrassing long time to finally reject Stalinism. I recall that, even later in Chicago, I would hang on my wall portraits of the "Big Five" (Marx, Engels, Lenin, Stalin, and Mao), which emotionally was no different than Christians' having a picture of Jesus or the Madonna hanging up. (I even got evicted from my apartment for doing this, for the Ukrainian landlady downstairs once had a look inside my apartment and took exception to the picture of Stalin – seems he had wiped out her family in the forced collectivization of agriculture of the early 1930's!)

On the other hand, I never did lose my political bearings in spite of the wild ride I was on, and I am proud that I stood alone in finally challenging CPC(M-L), as well as single-handedly preventing the liquidation of the Washington State Rainbow Coalition by Jesse Jackson in spite of the wishes of the other seven members of its state Executive Committee. But the antipathy of my former Partisan comrades when I fought against the CPC(M-L), as well as the reticence of the rest of the WSRC Executive Committee in my struggle with Jackson's liquidation attempt, makes me very leery of trusting the political judgment of others, particularly in a democratic centralist organization.

I may mention that, although I was very active in the Green Party for the past two decades at the local, state, and national levels, I have recently become inactive in that organization because of its evident inability to not try to get votes for its presidential candidate in swing states[10]. The political platform of the Green Party is excellent, but they can't seem to get around their (justified) antipathy towards the Democratic Party and their inflated sense of self-worth; a comrade has recently written to me that they exhibit "downright human insensitivity [towards the continued harm that Trump would do] on top of lousy politics".

Finally, let me close by relating an incident which demonstrates how crazy leftists can be. This was a rather vicious attack on me by a (former) friend in the Green Party of Seattle. He wrote the following on July 15, 2015 in response to my refusal to support Bernie Sanders during his 2016 presidential campaign because of his weak stand on Palestine:

"To not support Sanders in his growing movement to challenge the status quo is to expose oneself as a flaming hypocrite. Anyone who would say that people should not support Sanders because they disagree with him about one issue out of hundreds is just a mole, a liar, a plant working for the other side. Progressives have not had this sort of electoral potential in my lifetime. To argue against it and claim to be decent or honest is absurd. This is an important moment that no truly progressive person can or should resist endorsing."

Although he was right and I was wrong about the importance of Sanders's 2016 campaign, there is no excuse for his attacking me like this, especially since I actually had served as his treasurer in his 2010 campaign for U.S. Senate. (And this person is an academic, with a Ph.D. in Philosophy of Religion and Theology. I have no reason to doubt that he is highly rational.) Leftist politics can bring out the worst in people!

CHAPTER 5. CAPITALISM *vs.* SOCIALISM

a. The Socialist Economy

The British intellectual Ralph Miliband wrote a book[11] which presents in great detail a model for a socialist economy. It is a mixed economy which is considered to be the end goal which socialists should be striving for, not some sort of transitional society to a higher stage ("communism"?). I heartily endorse this model, and outline salient aspects of it here.

"A socialized economy would consist of three distinct sectors. First, there would be a predominant and varied public sector. Secondly, there would exist a substantial and expanding cooperative sector. Thirdly, there would endure a sizeable privately owned sector, mainly made up of small and medium firms, with an important part to play in the provision of goods, services, and amenities" (p. 110).

The public sector would include state ownership of the banking and financial system and of the immense corporations, which presently combine to control our political system for the benefit of the extremely wealthy ("the 1%"). State ownership ("nationalization") would be acquired not by outright confiscation, but through compensation "by way of the issue of government bonds, redeemable over an extended period of time; and a considerable degree of differentiation would also have to be made between small and large investors, with facilities for more rapid redemption available to small investors" (pp. 109-110).

Also included in the public sector would be regional and local activities undertaken by regional and municipal authorities, particularly in the provision of services and amenities such as transportation, electricity, water and sewage, daycare centers, and community centers, to name but a few such activities. Such economic activities are often already "owned" by the public, but under neoliberalism they are increasingly being privatized so that the wealthy can squeeze even more money out of the public.

Public enterprises would have a considerable degree of autonomy, unlike the bureaucratic Soviet system of rigid, top-down planning. Nonetheless, government would be able to intervene in their activities – sparingly applied – "to ensure compliance with its macro-economic policies and objectives, and with its concerns about health and safety, employment, and the rights of workers" (p. 110). Furthermore, there must be "the greatest possible degree of participation in the determination of policy by everyone employed in the enterprise who wishes to be involved, and the attribution of real power to employees in regard to all issues which directly affect them – for instance, health and safety, the process of production, conditions of work, etc." (p. 111).

Regarding the cooperative sector of a socialist economy, Miliband calls for the government to actively strengthen it, in the field of production as well as distribution, and in the provision of services. He points out that such enterprises now play a very subsidiary role in capitalist economies.

Finally, a sizeable sector would comprise a wide range of small and medium-sized firms, individually owned and controlled. Their existence would be considered to be a permanent feature of the socialist economy. Such private sector "introduces an additional element of competition in the provision of goods, services, and amenities. It gives the opportunity to individuals who are so inclined to ty their hand at independent ventures, and to experiment with new products and services. A socialist regime would not only find this acceptable, but would actively encourage such individual initiatives. But it would at the same time see to it that the private sector remained a subsidiary part of the economy as a whole" (p. 113).

All of these economic enterprises would be subject to competition from each other. "But market forces, in such an economy, would not be the ultimate determinant of economic life. The submission of the economy to unregulated market forces means the abdication by government and the society which sustains it of the responsibility for deciding what needs to be done for the common good and the achievements of social justice" (p. 117).

b. Why Choose Socialism?

Let us envision a conversation with a fully cognizant liberal or social democrat, with values compatible with ours but unwilling to supersede (U.S.) capitalism. She/he argues:

"Sure, you're absolutely right about the terrible harm which capitalism does to so many people, both at home and abroad. However, our goals are the same. But look at what results have been obtained when people try to overthrow capitalism. In Russia in 1917, communist revolutionaries overthrew nascent capitalism in that overwhelmingly peasant country, and in time established a brutal dictatorship over everyone including the working class which it was supposed to represent and enable politically. Its organizational success was repeated elsewhere (Eastern Europe, China, Vietnam) as outright one-party dictatorships, although Cuba at least has a government which well serves the needs of its people. Anti-capitalist revolutions naturally tend toward personal control by 'enlightened' leaders, as seen not only in monsters like Stalin and Pol Pot but also in the 'vanguard parties' which arose in the U.S. in the ferment of the 1970's, such as the Revolutionary Communist Party and the Communist Party (Marxist-Leninist). And these unassailable leaders often make major political mistakes.

"If you can claim, or hope, that all will better in a truly socialist society, I can just as well claim that it will be possible in time to overcome these deleterious effects of capitalism, although I realize that we are now in danger of the establishment of a highly authoritarian, even fascist, government through Trumpism. As Winston Churchill once remarked, (bourgeois) democracy is the least oppressive of the possible organization of society. People are mainly irrational, and collectively they can – and do - establish highly brutal societies in contradiction to what we both want."

I might respond by relating the manifold ways in which capitalism oppresses people, but she/he is already generally aware of them, so it would do no good. And in fact this argument in favor of maintaining capitalism is cogent, something which I might well have accepted as a budding academic had it not been for the unconscionable Vietnam War. But I can't accept it, not because the argument is faulty (which it isn't) but because I cannot tolerate the oppression which capitalism visits upon people – that is just the way I am, and this is an expression of the usual primacy of emotions over rational thought, as depicted in the figure for dialectical materialism. (And I'm not suggesting that I am in some sense morally superior to my interlocutor.) So it seems that, so far as rational thought goes, we are at a standoff concerning the need for socialism.

APENNDIX A

Statement published in the May 28, 1964 issue of the *New York Herald Tribune* and signed by 150 persons:

We the undersigned

Are young Americans of draft age. We understand our obligations to defend our country and to serve in the armed forces but we object to being asked to support the war in South Vietnam.

Believing that United States participation in that war is for suppression of the Vietnamese struggle for national independence, we see no justification for our involvement. We agree with Senator Wayne Morse, who said on the floor of Senate on March 4, 1964, regarding South Vietnam, that "We should never have gone in. We should never have stayed in. We should get out."

Believing that we should not be asked to fight against the people of Vietnam, we herewith state our refusal to do so.

APPENDIX B

(This poem was published in the documents of the founding convention of the Progressive Labor Party, in 1965.)

How to be a good communist
by Les Turner

Feel

the millions unwilling to die without living, wanting to
     BE without begging, trying and learning,
     demanding, organizing.

Feel

the children bred for dying, wasting in gutters, skinny-
     diseased-bleeding from wounds inflicted by hands
     not feeling, facing, not knowing a time without
     suffering.

Feel

the bombs now falling on women still carrying unborn
     slaves of selfishness, the greed ever-growing
     digesting the living, spitting out the piths.

Feel

the shanty serfdom shit houses, shacks serving as
     home for servants, indentured to the cause of
     inhumanity.

Feel

the spirits crushed by destroyers cruising, always
     threatening, rolling Freedom in their wake.

Feel

the cold dungeon's dampness felt each second by the
        damned who did speak and they became victims
        of the way still too weak to stand.
Feel
the surge of unrest pounding in the varicose veins of
        the people
Feel
the fire igniting the strengthening arms of the militant
Feel
the almost uncollapsible coldness, the wall of
        oppression
Feel
the muffled roar of the martyrs
Feel
the freedom coming
Feel
the unrest pounding
the fire igniting
the roar still sounding
the freedom coming
the people marching
Feel, feel, feel
and join the marchers
become one with the masses
attend THEIR classes
the wall collapsing
learn the song sung by the people
on the poles of the nation
- Having done this
Shall the People call us Communist!

APENNDIX C

The following is the first draft of my "Moving Forward" column scheduled for publication in the August 2020 issue of the newspaper *Works in Progress* of Olympia, Washington.:

Is President Donald Trump leading us into fascism? To consider this question, it is necessary to understand the role which fascism plays in a capitalist society, why the capitalist class turns to facilitating the rise of fascism. Such understanding is provided in the collection of essays **Radical Perspectives on the Rise of Fascism in Germany, 1919-1945** (Monthly Review Press, 1989).

In the aftermath of World War I, a democratic parliamentary political system was set up in defeated Germany, as the "Weimar Republic". The capitalists were divided into three major factions: heavy industry (iron, steel, mining) focused on domestic economic development; export industry (dynamic, technologically more advanced, and more prosperous) led by machine, electric, and chemical industries as well as textiles and commercial interests; and agriculture (the landed aristocracy, particularly the "Junkers" of Prussia). The "middle class" consisted of shopkeepers, commodity producers, and salaried employees, as well as the peasantry). The working class had strong labor unions and a strong political party (the Social Democratic Party of Germany, or

"SPD") and a German Communist Party ("KPD") which had been greatly weakened by the abortive revolutionary uprisings following World War I.

At first the export-industry fraction of the bourgeoisie was dominant in representing capital, and the labor unions and SPD were able to work with this fraction in considerably improving workers' lives, until 1930. They were, in fact, "too" successful, for heavy industry was then unable to make a decent profit and the economic system was in major distress. In the early 1930's heavy industry achieved hegemony over the export industry and refused to collaborate politically with workers' organizations. However, the political system was so dysfunctional that the Weimar parliament lost most mass support in spite of efforts by heavy industry to revive it. The only really strong political parties in the early 1930's were the fascist NSDAP (the National Socialist German Workers Party of Hitler, based most strongly in the "middle class") and the SPD (with some help from the KPD, although at this time the communists were denouncing the social democrats as being the main enemy of the revolution). So the capitalists tried to use the NSDAP as a junior partner in parliament, as a substitute for their lack of mass following. But Hitler refused any deal other than one making him Chancellor, and the capitalists finally capitulated, especially since the NSDAP in the most recent election appeared to be in decline and there was the danger that it would fade away.

So on January 30, 1933 Hitler was appointed Chancellor of Germany. He quickly destroyed the labor unions and soon all other political parties, using as necessary the huge army of streetfighters (the SA, or "stormtroopers") which the NSDAP had built up. Through a referendum he had himself and his party declared the sole ruler of Germany, and by 1938 he had replaced the old state bureaucracy with his own followers. Anti-
Semitism was eagerly implemented in Germany, with Jews deprived of any political or social influence and even of their livelihood; this treatment was but a prelude to the Holocaust which the Germans carried out in eastern Europe as soon as they were able to, when Germany invaded Poland in September 1939.

Furthermore, analysis for understanding authoritarianism in the United States aids in comprehending the possibilities for implementing fascism here. A comrade has kindly provided the following analysis of authoritarianism here, the key reference points being slavery, the Civil War, the rollback of Reconstruction, Jim Crow, and changing demographics as a major stress for the contemporary period. The next column will then consider the question of to what extent Trump is implementing fascism in the United States.

In the pre-Civil-War period and the Civil War, a whole section of society, anchored in the slaveowners but extending to a cross-class white bloc, viewed their whole civilization and "way of life" as being dependent on maintaining slavery. So they used "any means necessary" to try to defend and expand it. They were beaten, but came back via racist terror and the assault on Black voting rights to roll back Reconstruction and put in place Jim Crow for a hundred years. This was essentially apartheid – Blacks in the South "had no rights the white man needed to respect" and this was enforced through lynching – *i.e.* through open terror.

Now we are living through another stage in the rollback of the gains of the 1960's (and of the 30's as well). And for the first time since the Civil War, a whole layer of society – again rooted in the most reactionary sectors of capital but extending to a cross-class white bloc – believes (since because of demographic change, the U.S. in 30-40 years will be a majority people-of-color country) that if democracy and majority rule exists in the U.S., their whole way of life (white Christian American civilization) will go under. So they are prepared to – more than that, enthusiastic to – set in place a system for long-term rule by a minority of the population via authoritarian means. Big sectors of capital – not all, but highly important ones such as energy corporations and the military-industrial complex – are behind this because they know their ecoholic and energy policies (climate change denialism) are unpopular not just with communities of color but also with young whites.

So there is a massive force moving toward what could be called neo-apartheid, a racialized authoritarian state, "illiberal democracy" or even a not-classical-European fascism but still essentially a form of fascism. This may occur even in the absence of a strong communist or revolutionary left. This is what Trumpism is about: the absolute determination of roughly 30% of the U.S. population right now to turn to explicit authoritarianism in which immigrants and Blacks are not "real Americans" and have no rights that the "real Americans" need to respect.

APPENDIX D

The following is the first draft of my "Moving Forward" column scheduled for publication in the October 2020 issue of the newspaper *Works in Progress* of Olympia, Washington.:

[This draft may have to be updated as the time for publication (October) approaches.]

Is President Donald Trump promoting fascism in the United States? With the previous column's understanding of the rise of fascism in Germany and the history of authoritarianism in our own country, let us first look at the ways in which it is valid to say that Trump is doing this:

1. Trump is building up a mass following based on explicit calls for white supremacy. (The Republican Party has long been implicitly based on white supremacy, starting with Nixon's "Southern strategy"; he is raising use of this noxious ideology to a new level.)

2. Another critical component of building a mass reactionary following is Trump's clearly stated misogyny.

3. Trump viciously attacks "The Other", in this case immigrants of color and Moslems. This corresponds with the Nazis's using Jews and Slavs (non-Aryans) as their scapegoats.

4. Trump expresses utter contempt for persons who oppose or disagree with him.

5. Trump engages in blatant lying, knowing full well that doing this will be accepted by his mass base.

6. Trump attacks the mass media, whether conservative or liberal, as "the enemy of the people".

7. Trump dismisses as "fake news" whatever evidence contradicts his pronouncements, including undeniable scientific conclusions. Thus with this and the preceding three points he has been building up a mass of followers who mindlessly accept whatever pronouncement he chooses to make.

8. Trump completely disregards the rule of law whenever it suits him. In fact, early in his tenure he stated that if he were voted out of office, he might have to obey the wishes of his followers in their insistence that he remain in office.

On the other hand, there are important ways in which Trump does not go beyond staunch conservatism towards outright fascism:

1. Trump is not building up a disciplined mass party like Hitler's NSDAP.

2. Trump is not creating organized militias like the Nazis's SA stormtroopers.

3. Trump has little support of much of the major economic elite. They are not yet needing him as

Supreme Leader with mass support, as heavy industry did in the early 1930's in Germany.

4. Trump gives strong support for military spending, but not for entanglement in foreign wars. (One of the few positive things that one can say about Trump's conduct!)

5. Trump gives strong support for maintenance of the U.S. empire, especially regarding Israel, but this is what the Republicans and mainstream Democrats do anyway.

6. Trump provides basically nominal support for Christian conservatism, but not including blatant religious fervor such as that expressed in anti-Semitism.

7. Trump also provides nominal support for anti-LGBTQ activity, but not to the extent of making such persons "The Other".

So what can one conclude from this analysis? It would be wrong to charge Trump with systematically bringing about fascism, for that is only going to happen when a fundamental economic crisis occurs and the economic elite find it necessary to use the mass base provided by demagogues like Trump to destroy our outwardly democratic processes in order to effect a fascist dictatorship. But it *is* reasonable to recognize that Trump is laying the *groundwork* (even if unintentionally) for a future transformation to fascism. This, as well as Trump's vigorous promotion

of climate change which will destroy the world, is why
it is so critically important to deny him a second term
in office. (And the need for a fascist dictatorship may
be forthcoming sooner than one might think, for
neoliberalism is sinking capitalism into the ground
with no alternative in sight.)

APPENDIX E:

Dave Jette, "Viewpoint: Defeating Trump".
November/December 2019. Published in *Against the
Current* (magazine of the socialist organization
Solidarity): https://solidarity-us.org/atc/203/defeat-
trump/:

In her recent Viewpoint article in this magazine,
"What Sanders' Campaign Opens", Dianne Feeley
very well describes the possibilities which Bernie
Sanders's pursuit of the Democratic Party's 2020
presidential nomination opens up for socialists. I agree
with this presentation, but I think that it incorrectly
omits the critical need to defeat Donald Trump next
year even if we have to actively support a more
mainstream Democrat for this purpose.

There are two basic reasons for what may be for
some a shocking proposition: first, Trump is
systematically, and with considerable success, bringing
about fascism in our country; and second, he is
destroying whatever defenses we presently have to
help avoid the climate change which will be
catastrophic for the whole world. This suggested
course of action would certainly have been shocking to
me until very recently, for until then I had been
adamant in rejecting any collusion with the
Democratic Party, realizing that it like the Republican
Party is a creature of the 1% and that its role for
countless decades has been to emasculate and absorb
any serious challenge to their rule; attempts to
"capture" and transform the Democratic Party into one

serving the needs of the vast majority of our populace have been demonstrated, time and time again, to be a fool's errand. Nonetheless, the political situation with which we are now faced is so grave that it is imperative to do whatever is possible to deprive Trump of an even more devasting second term of office – we simply cannot avoid to stick our heads in the sand and hope that things work out for the better.

Regarding Ms. Feeley's article, I am less pessimistic than she about the prospect of Sanders's garnering the Democratic Party's nomination – he's running a highly active grassroots-based campaign, and he may be able to pull it off in spite of the Party's leadership. But more to the point is the refusal of the Democratic Socialists of America, through a resolution passed at their national convention in August, to support any Democratic Party presidential candidate other than Sanders. Her take on that decision seems to be supportive, pointing out that it demonstrates that Sanders's candidacy doesn't trap individuals and organizations inside the Democratic Party. My own take is rather different, that it is highly dismaying, demonstrating that DSA is not yet able to do that which is absolutely necessary at this time, i.e. to work as hard as possible to prevent Trump's continuation as president. It's fine and dandy to have strongly socialist politics, but not if your (well justified) antipathy to the Democratic Party results in your dropping the ball.

I've been highly active in the Green Party for many years, serving as treasurer for its electoral campaigns at all levels including for federal office. As usual, the Green Party will be running a candidate for president next year, and it was therefore natural for me to come up with a proposed set of objectives for its candidate's campaign, keeping in mind the overriding necessity of defeating Trump while also not watering down its own excellent political stance. I came up with the following four points:

1. The presidential campaign should encourage everyone to defeat Trump by voting for the Democratic Party nominee in any state in which the race is at all close, and to help get out the vote in those states. The Green Party should become clearly identified with the struggle to prevent a second term for Trump and substantially contribute to defeating him.

2. The campaign should support the campaigns of local Green Party candidates, as the necessary first step in building the party. Running presidential and statewide candidates with no chance of winning is basically a waste of time and energy.

3. The campaign should promote the Green Party as a genuine progressive electoral party, which will occur naturally through promotion of the first two objectives, as well as in campaigning in the absence of local Green Party candidates. On the one hand it will establish the political maturity of the Party through its active and highly public involvement in the effort to dump Trump, and on the other hand it will be advocating a full progressive political platform for serious consideration.

4. The campaign should still seek to get a high vote
   total for the Green Party presidential candidate.
   Although this will be a secondary objective
   contingent upon satisfying the first three objectives,
   it is still desirable to demonstrate substantial voter
   support in states in which it cannot possibly hinder
   ousting Trump.

The foregoing objectives could of course apply
for any progressive third-party presidential campaign,
but my intention was to convince the Green Party (at
its presidential nominating convention next July) to
approve this course of action for its nominee. But after
investigating prospects for such approval, I've been
convinced that there is no chance of this being
obtained, and I have accordingly decided to no longer
be wasting my time and to withdraw from active
participation in the Green Party, which evidently has
no capability of becoming the sort of progressive
electoral party which is so needed. The reader may be
interested in my article "Relation of Progressives to
the Democratic Party" which was published in the July
2019 issue of Works in Progress of Olympia,
Washington; it is available at
https://olywip.org/relation-of-progressives-to-the-
democratic-party.

APPENDIX F

Dave Jette, "9/11 and Nationalism". Published in the August 2018 issue of *Works in Progress*, Olympia, Washington: www.olywip.org/book-review-9-11-and-nationalism/.

This is a review of *9/11 Ten Years Later: When State Crimes Against Democracy Succeed* by David Ray Griffin (Olive Branch Press, 2011). The book demonstrates that the 9/11 attacks on the Twin Towers of the World Trade Center and on the Pentagon were an inside job, a false flag operation. The attacks did not, as claimed by the Bush administration and the mass media, result from a conspiracy carried out by operatives of al-Qaeda under the direction of Osama bin Laden.

An inside job

The idea that these horrendous attacks were carried out by elements of our own government is surely frightening. What is even more frightening is the total, mindless rejection by the great majority of Americans of this as an inside job that our enlightened country could never do. This appeal to nationalism as the basic faith of Americans is what I consider to be the most important understanding provided by the book, but let me first outline the author's proofs that there was a government conspiracy.

A coherent case relying on evidence

The bulk of this book is devoted to demonstrating, in great detail, the impossibility of the government's al-Qaeda conspiracy theory. Ten years after 9/11, Griffin has sorted through the relevant facts and opinions to produce a coherent case against the official explanation of what happened. The reader herself/himself will need to read the book to evaluate the veracity of the points he makes (pp. 27-50 for the WTC buildings) as well as the whole of his analysis. We can here mention only some of his salient points:

1. The twin towers were not brought down by the airliners which penetrated them. The official story is that the fires fueled by the jet fuel aboard the aircraft melted the steel supporting the top floors of each tower (and throughout the structure), causing the top floors to fall and take the rest of the building with them. But the melting point of steel is 2800°F, whereas these fires could not have been hotter than 1800°F -- the maximum possible temperature for hydrocarbon-based building fires. Previously, there have been no incidents of such fires bringing down steel-framed high rises, even in the case of examples cited by Griffin of much larger, destructive fires.

2. There were also huge horizontal ejections of steel from the twin towers, which could only have been caused by explosives, not by the fires.

3. A third World Trade Center building (WTC7) collapsed that day. It was very large (47 stories), and it came down some six hours after the twin towers (WTC1 and WTC2). It came down in the short time required for absolute free fall, which -- according to the laws of physics (conservation of momentum and conservation of energy) -- could not have resulted from the top floors collapsing and bringing down the remaining floors. (I happen to be a physicist, with a Ph.D. in theoretical physics, and I was able to calculate and confirm that the collapse time was too short for the building to have collapsed solely under the weight of the top floors.) Moreover, the building collapsed directly into its footprint, symmetrically (straight down, with an almost perfectly horizontal roofline), which indicates that its base supporting steel columns were *all* destroyed at once.

4. Civil engineering experts thus concluded that all three WTC buildings were brought down by controlled demolitions. There was clear evidence of the presence of nanothermite (which can be tailored to behave as an incendiary or an explosive) in the WTC dust. In fact the WTC debris continued burning for six months -- impossible for ordinary building materials, but explained by the presence of nanothermite.

5. A number of calls reported from passengers on the doomed aircrafts were demonstrated to have

been fake. Some calls couldn't have been made using cell phones at such a high altitude, and the seatback telephones had been made inoperative for a number of months by the airline.

6. The official story claims that a Boeing 757 flown by al-Qaeda's Hani Hanjour crashed into the Pentagon. However, his flight school judged Hanjour to be incompetent to fly even a single-engine aircraft. Whatever hit the Pentagon took an extremely difficult trajectory which would have tested even a highly experienced pilot. (But not to worry, for evidently the target was achieved: where the Pentagon was struck there were no high-ranking Pentagon officials. Instead, the personnel carrying out an investigation into several billion dollars of unaccounted funds, as well as the relevant records, were wiped out.)

7. Although Osama bin Laden immediately denied involvement in the 9/11 attacks and continued to do so, the US military "found" a video of him admitting responsibility. How they found it was never made clear, and it appears to have been bogus. Rather than capturing bin Laden and bringing him to trial, the U.S. military murdered him nine years later. By disposing of his body by burial at sea, they avoided any Muslim friends or acquaintances being able to identify him. (It's even probable that they killed someone else, for

bin Laden had been in poor health and quite
likely had already died.)

Griffin reports that while there is no consensus among the critics of the government's 9/11 conspiracy theory as to what actually hit the Pentagon, there is agreement that the WTC buildings were brought down by controlled demolition.

Obstructing an investigation, blaming al-Qaeda

The Bush administration did everything it could to prevent an investigation into 9/11. They appointed political operatives to executive positions in the 9/11 Commission (first attempting, unsuccessfully, to install Henry Kissinger as its Chairman!) and drastically underfunded the Commission's work. Vice-President Dick Cheney (not a Commission member) was, in fact, directly implicated in the attacks through his failure to order the military to shoot down the aircraft approaching the Pentagon. The 9/11 Commission produced the required report blaming al-Qaeda for the attacks.

The 9-11 Truth Movement

But as it became increasingly clear that the 9/11 attacks had been an inside job employing controlled demolition, the 9/11 Truth Movement was formed. It included many distinguished professionals from various fields (pp. 57-59 and pp. 222-226): former

State Department officials, intelligence agency officials (including the CIA), and high-ranking military leaders as well as over 1500 architects and engineers in Architects and Engineers for 9/11 Truth. Their conclusion was that the attacks had been an inside job employing controlled demolition.

Failure of the mass media

However, the mass media in our country (but not elsewhere in the world) almost completely ignored the objections to the government's conspiracy theory. This is hardly surprising since our mass media as well as our federal government is controlled by the 1%, in whose interest was the subsequent invasion of and attacks upon oil-rich Muslim countries. (Some months before 9/11, our government had decided to create "regime change" in Afghanistan, Iran, Iraq, Libya, Somalia, and Yemen, and 9/11 gave it a widely accepted excuse to do so in its subsequent "War on Terrorism".) So mainstream opinion-makers commonly described members of the 9/11 Truth Movement as nuts, cranks, and idiots, as mindless advocates of conspiracy theories. (Of course, there are two conspiracy theories involved here, the government's blaming al-Qaeda and the 9/11 Truth Movement's blaming the government. But the mass media recognizes and dismisses derisively only the latter "conspiracy theory".)

The U.S. as the indispensable nation for good in the world

Also dismissing critics of the government's conspiracy theory out-of-hand were leftist intellectuals like Noam Chomsky, Alexander Cockburn, and Bill Moyers, as well as the great majority of Americans. Why would so many people refuse to examine seriously the evidence and arguments of the 9/11 Truth Movement? Chapter 8 of the book explains that what is operative here is nationalist faith. This (rather than Christianity, for example) is the basic faith of Americans: that the United States is the exception country, the indispensable country, for advancing civilization throughout the world. This faith rests on the belief that we are fundamentally a virtuous nation and, while we occasionally may make major mistakes (such as in Vietnam and Iraq), we are essentially good, never deliberately doing anything terribly evil. Surely our government could never kill some 2800 Americans for political purposes!

I admit that I succumbed to this outlook, at least partially. Right after 9/11, I was aware of criticisms of the official story, but I thought "who other than al-Qaeda might have carried out the attacks?".

Identifying a possible perpetrator

To answer this question, I listed five requirements for a possible alternate perpetrator:

requisite technical expertise, political motivation (in terms of goals for the future), opportunity (ability to do what was practically necessary), expectation of being shielded from any exposure or retribution, and the will (ethics) to sacrifice so many people. With these criteria I deduced that the only possible alternate perpetrator would have to be … Israel. I eliminated the United States since I didn't think that our government could possibly carry out such a heinous act against its own people.

But since then, I've read *JFK and the Unspeakable: Why He Died and Why It Matters* by James W. Douglass (2010). Douglas demonstrates definitively how President Kennedy was assassinated by what we term the Deep State (here, mainly the CIA but also including elements of the military and the Secret Service). Through Griffin's book I have now studied and understood the 9/11 attacks. I have concluded that it was not Israel (because of the complexity of the operation) but the "Deep State" that carried out the 9/11 attacks.

The Deep State and our nationalist faith

So where does this understanding leave us? We do have to be cognizant of the existence of the Deep State, rather than allowing it to be dismissed as just another "conspiracy theory" (derisively, in scare quotation marks). The Deep State intervenes on

matters of critical importance to "national security,"
viz. the maintenance and expansion of the Empire.

More importantly, we have to understand the immense hold that nationalist faith has on Americans, in facilitating their support of our enormous military spending and of our imperialist wars throughout the world. We are well aware of the role of white nationalism (in the form of white supremacy) in our country, but the problem goes much deeper. An overwhelming nationalism pervades our society, evinced by the strong support for Donald Trump's call to "make America first" even among those who are not rabid white supremacists.

Some progressives will say that we shouldn't get bogged down in questioning the government's 9/11 story, that we should instead concentrate on more immediate matters facing us. But it is our duty to make people aware of what exactly is going on so that they can themselves decide what course of action to take, rather than deciding for them what information would be useful to them. If and when fascism comes to the United States, it will be on the basis of nationalism rather than simply white supremacy and conservative Christianity, and progressives should know what to expect and guard against.

ENDNOTES

1. Joe Lieberman served as a U.S. Senator from Connecticut for eighteen years, commencing in 1989, and ran for vice-president on the Democratic ticket in 2000. He supported some progressive struggles, such as for abortion rights and repeal of the military's "Don't ask, don't tell" policy, but he critically opposed having a public option in the Affordable Care Act ("Obamacare"). He was a hawk concerning foreign policy, supporting American military action against Grenada, Libya, Panama, Kosovo, Afghanistan, Iraq, Iran, Syria, and Yemen. He also supported the suppression of civil liberties in the name of national security, including suppression of Wikileaks.

2. Paul Wolfowitz served as U.S. Deputy Secretary of Defense from 2001-2005, and played a major role in promoting U.S. attacks on Iraq and Afghanistan during that period.

3. There have been many books written about the Kennedy assassination, mostly incomplete and sometimes giving false information. I have found incontrovertible and complete **JFK and the Unspeakable: Why He Died and Why It Matters** by James W. Douglass (2008). This book explains in full detail how the "Deep State" murdered Kennedy, the Deep State being the

highest levels of our security apparatus (CIA, FBI, Secret Service, military) which intervenes when the Empire is acutely threatened by U.S. politicians. Although many progressives prefer to ignore it and hide their heads in the sand, the Deep State actually carried out the 9/11 attacks, as explained in Appendix F.

4. There were other factors accelerating the Partisan Organization's demise, include the need of its top leadership (not including me) to avoid being replaced because of major organizational errors. I published a lengthy analysis of the experience of the Partisan Organization in *Theoretical Review* #13 (November-December 1979) of the Tucson Marxist-Leninist Collective. This article, entitled "The Partisan Experience", is on pages 41-46, and its author (me) is not identified.

5. **A Reformulation of Dialectical Materialism** by Dave Jette. Self-published in 2019 and available from Lulu.com in soft-cover ($9) and hard-cover ($19) editions.

6. **Radiation Therapy Physics**, edited by Alfred R. Smith (Springer-Verlag, 1995): Chapter 5, "Electron Beam Dose Calculations", by David Jette (pages 95-121).

7. From the Preface to **A Contribution to the Critique of Political Economy**, by Karl Marx, 1859.

8. Max Elbaum, **Revolution in the Air** (second edition, Verso, 2018).

9. **The Rosa Luxemburg Reader**, edited by Peter Hudis & Kevin B. Anderson (Monthly Review Press, 2004): p. 302 from "The Russian Revolution" written in September 2018,

10. Ralph Miliband, **Socialism for a Sceptical Age** (Verso, 1994).

www.ingramcontent.com/pod-product-compliance
Lightning Source LLC
Chambersburg PA
CBHW072308270726
48657CB00030B/908